PHILLY ROULETTE

THE

GAMBLE THAT FAILED

MELVING PRINCE JOHNAKIN

HOLLIS MEDIA GROUP
PUBLISHER

Melvin Prince Johnakin

Melvin Prince Johnakin

CONTENTS

DEDICATION 6

FOREWORD 8

CHAPTER 1 I Am My Brother's Keeper 11

CHAPTER 2 Ideal Partner 21

CHAPTER 3 Is This Shit Real 38

CHAPTER 4 Don't Believe Your Lying Eyes 51

CHAPTER 5 Some Gambles were Duds 62

CHAPTER 6 The Perfect Dichotomy 77

CHAPTER 7 The Culture 87

ABOUT THE AUTHOR 102

DEDICATION

This Book is Dedicated to: Ms. Trellie Johnakin, my beloved mother and the President of Schuylkill Falls Tenant Council. She would always say; "Don't talk about it, be about it!", Marvin Dunmeyer, my best friend at Schuylkill Falls. I was the number two Guard and he was the Big Small Forward, and Kenneth Hayward aka "Big Champ", known as the "Glue" of Schuylkill Falls. He always wanted the best for every resident in Schuylkill Falls.

Last but not least, to my amazing two sons: To Josiah my youngest son who is very smart and has the best smile in the world (you will lead many). And to my oldest son Kevin who is very strong and has the best wisdom and focus that is better than most older men (nothing is impossible). My apologies Josiah Johnakin and Kevin Bradley.

THE PUN

GAME CHANGERS, BALLERS, the ones with notable success; those with DRIP (swag), that possess the epitome of fierce tenacity and relentless drive to succeed who often seem luckier than others or having the magic touch for everything where there is *"NO STOPPING US"*;   occasionally rolls the dice one too many or summons the majestic twirl of the ROULETTE wheel and finds out the hard way that sometimes there is that GAMBLE that fails.

FOREWORD

Since the ratification of the Housing and Urban Development Act of 1968, residents of public housing were to have been afforded economic development, entrepreneurship and self-sufficiency opportunities in order to eradicate the vicious cycle of multi-generational poverty, disenfranchisement and social destruction. It's unfortunate that the vision of the Lyndon B. Johnson Administration in the historic legislation that was passed has yet to be realized some 50 years later. Residents of public housing continue to be exposed to crime, violence, and limited educational and economic development opportunities. Furthermore, housing contains the highest proportion of able-bodied unemployed individuals than any other demographic group in the United States. This phenomenon has proven deleterious on our youth and family structure.

To bring the original vision to light the community at Schuylkill Falls, one of Philadelphia's Public Housing Developments, adopted a philosophy of "improved self-sufficiency." This theory is realized by harnessing the powers of the human spirit, ingenuity, education, and courage to achieve economic stability, wealth creation, and educational opportunities for our residents. It involves the establishment of private partnerships to facilitate the capital needs of our Resident-Owned and Operated Businesses.

The following contains the most rewarding initiative ever tried and completed by a Public Housing community – the successful implementation and lifelong wealth creation strategies for all of our residents and the resurgence of our community as a jewel for economic, educational, cultural and social stability for the 21st Century, and beyond.

I am most honored and humbled that the residents of Schuylkill Falls allowed me to lead this grand experience. I am grateful to everyone who assists us in the perfection of this strategy and vision.

May God continue to bless us and lead us in our pursuit!

Mrs. Trellie Johnakin
Tenant Council President
7/25/2005

"... are we there yet...did we hit the mark? - keep reading"

INTRODUCTION

I cannot make this up, the stories are just too darn spectacular but unfortunately true. This book is not one that I wrote without much soul searching, or reflection; it is a story that has to be told because too many are sold out in the name of social services, namely a provider or manager of housing projects whereby the very institution is a death trap for most.

Melvin Prince Johnakin

1

AM I MY BROTHER'S KEEPER?

The compelling argument is we are indeed part of a bigger construct in life; we are assigned to help, to lead, to provide and nurture others... it is a fundamental principle of humanity to exchange and make a difference for those who need us. In addition, it is the same mantra of being there for others than many have mistaken the spirit of it and forgotten about individual responsibility and participation to their detriment.

How many times have we heard the vernacular: "I gottcha man; with me at the helm all is good. And that means you good!" Actually, the metaphor means absolutely nothing when the "Stalwarts", society's nobility is enshrined in the lowest of all con games that impacts the poor, frail and forgotten, "Human Services".

The weak, the underprivileged, and sometimes uneducated become the bait that feeds the underworld of greed and supported by so many but in the spirit of love.

On paper billions are set aside from taxation to create safety nets and provide basic human services to keep our brother and sister from total collapse; at least this is what it says on paper. But what we do know is the very construct of the system primarily feeds and stuffs the belly of a bottomless unrepentant beast whose appetite is exclusively obsessed on MORE, MORE, MORE. The access given to the establishment and its cohorts provides a privilege to drink from faucets that run constantly but their thirst is never quenched. The idealistic promise of always having a safeguard, a big brother to look out for you if one should ever need a helping hand became one the biggest frauds in modern history. And still remains hidden in plain sight.

For those without anything, a home, money, a support network the institution is the savior. However, the end result for more than a few became a graveyard that buried the hopes and dreams of GOD's CREATION. Individuals that never realized their worth to change the world but were beaten down and mentally ensnared to just accept a little. You know, something is better than nothing.

Unknowingly for those financially dependent on the "SYSTEM" once in, it is akin to entering the doorway of no return. They are placed in a pool that is at best a "MURKY watering hole that drowns out life and vitality" though the hierarchy of needs are being met; housing, and all the wrap around services that come with it: Food Stamps, Medical, Vision Care, Dental, and Vouchers for school lunches. Yet, the backdrop is a tapestry of unknowns, a playground for corruption where the gatekeepers live in glass houses that never break...a well-designed IDEA guarded by legislative decrees that are at best empty promises.

The gatekeepers personify good will, the elite trusts them to carry out the People's business because it is too messy from the top to be so intimately visible because it might show their hand and how the money flows. So, it is imperative to shroud the needs of the many in conversations and pass provision through legislation to keep the bills paid, and that entails having a guardian. "My Brother's Keeper". A point man or person that the people like. One who can convince the downtrodden they are the Knight in shining armor, the gateway to a better future..

What many never realize is this is just a gamble to the elite, possibly a sure bet because it keeps their hands cleaner. Noticed I did not say clean.

Having an intermediary helps to clean up loose ends and eliminates direct exposure because the vast playground where the elite romp and tout themselves as leaders, and patriots of humanity is littered with tempered minds that are conditioned not to want or seek more... after all the trough from which they eat is managed by the BIG hog himself that ain't going nowhere. He's the native son and has nothing but love for the people and ain't nothing stopping his magnetism and finesse to continue feeding from the trough. See he knows the insufficiency of the least is the most covenant meal ticket he would ever need, and the money is well stocked. And he is well liked, unassuming... a safe bet.

LET'S TAKE ANOTHER LOOK...

However, here is the dichotomy; the "Working Class", the "Rich" often frown upon and discount the value of struggling families entrapped in the very "system" that feeds their lavish lifestyle. The low/no income person is often seen and labeled a "liability"; inept and lazy. Just a burden to the collective, but it is the same system that herds the needy to an unforeseeable future where many die without ever seeing the world. Though it was their plight that built careers and perpetuated back door deals at taxpayer's expense.

Of course, no one seems to want to educate themselves about the business behind the business of human services. I guess it is easier to blame the least because to the naked eye everything is handed to them, but for those feeding from that same channel the labeling is often of eloquent adjectives.

The Adage "NOTHING IS FREE" is explicitly just that, NOT FREE. The good that many receive doesn't merely come from the hearts of those with more compassion or from a desire to see humankind elevated to a quality lifestyle. Sometimes the good is generated by a system designed to rape the soul of ambition and perpetuate the "sin" of dependency and curse of *"poverty"*; though it affords the masterminds that have figured out the formula to stay in position and to pillage payrolls, while manipulating contracts as a means to pay for college, stash away a nest egg, acquire a second home, drive expensive cars, and other ill-gotten benefits stolen from the "PEOPLE", and in the context of helping... human services.

The "UNSUSPECTING" beneficiaries have no clue that the mouse trap is the glue strip built not merely to capture, but to totally dominate them to use as pawns to milk the system that allows a select few INTELLECTUAL architects to create a lifestyle of luxury. The misfortune of the masses is the table from which nobility dines... those without anything became the collateral that made others rich and expanded their lineage of wealth while the broken, the poor and overlooked were the dividends that made it possible.

Human Services is the anchor that touches every person with a conscience, even the profiteers and vultures. The predators that lurk for the weak and vulnerable know if only they can keep the numbers consistently flowing, the billables are guaranteed. It's the easy meal in plain sight(*the poor you have with you always*) because it's all a numbers game. The more we create dependency the legacy of others is sustained.

Melvin Prince Johnakin

So, if you ever wondered why the system has never cancelled a contract for government housing though Congress, mostly Republicans, holler about doing away with Welfare, one president tried his darned best to reform it, but not the BIG BUSINESS behind it. Literally who do you think will vote for that? Definitely not the UNIONS. Too many service contracts – thousands eat from the trough that stretches in places none would ever think to look.

So why are we here? Great question, and lots of answers, but I'll sum it up; arrogance fueled by greed. Those placed in charge are/were not necessarily qualified, insightful, or caring, just well known. It was the cancerous ruse of presumption that led to what many thought would be a safe bet, though risky. However, the POWERS-that-BE placed a wager on the gambler that came from nothing: no formal education, a former resident of the housing projects. But someone who made a name for himself and put the CITY of BROTHERLY LOVE on a global map though under a different umbrella. And it was widely reported that he pillaged his private contracts then and I guess most would conclude it was that very mindset that created this conundrum.... He took because he could. He stole because he could... He Gambled and won a few, but the spinning wheel this time may land differently.

With that said, it would not be completely unthinkable to presume a person that escaped the trappings of staunch poverty, public housing, and attended inadequate schools though he did not graduate, would be the best candidate to lead government funded initiatives worth hundreds of millions. Projects that are part of a vast supply-chain and impacts hundreds of thousands of low/no income citizens though the original creation was to be "temporary". YOU know, until one could get themselves together; get a better a job or increase their education (knowledge base), take up a vocation to qualify for better employment.

So, since we're still inquiring, and taking another glance at a process one could ask: Shouldn't such a sacred trust of human well-being be conferred upon businesses and trained professionals with experience for the task at hand? One whose CV speaks of milestones and fiscal accountability; once again, with some reference to the very industry he or she is requesting to participate in? Or is it easier to find/or accept the knock at the door from enthusiasts who heard about the money on the table, because they were sitting around the table where conversations were shared about big business opportunities with the government, though the inquirer is sometimes without the acumen to participate, but just knows somebody? It's just a question.

Melvin Prince Johnakin

When it comes to serving the poor there are countless loopholes and cutting corners that nobody seems to care about between private/public partnerships. Mistakenly or maybe not, the gate is open to wild dogs salivating at the thought of the next no bid contract to manage the interest of the forgotten. You know after all "they are doing them a favor".

We should never confuse the two: Private money could be spent without any accountability if so be it the executive oversight is allowed to squander it. But this becomes totally UNACCEPTABLE when public funding (taxpayers) are footing the bills. We are shareholders and demand accountability and transparency from those in charge... otherwise, they must go!

In addition, though a slogan can say a lot, and often eludes to excellence and transformation ("Promoting Opportunities for Positive Community Change") as the driving message. However, it is in no way the actualization of creating and implementing effective procedures and policies that directly empowers recipients to get out of the rut and manifest change. Often times these subgroups are vacuums for waste and fraud, and sadly a vehicle to steal in plain sight with the help of friends in high places, and those who prey on them.

We have been knocking on the door of injustice for a long time, tapping nicely to let us in to clean up, to restore hope and create better solutions but without any success. However, now is the time we will kick the door down and play at the table of JUSTICE, because like Philly, America cannot afford another GAMBLE that failed.

Melvin Prince Johnakin

2

IDEAL PARTNER

Fundamentally, every business venture that involves two or more people requires and demands specific levels of expertise and strategic vision in order to thrive; there is no faking it! If the plan is to succeed beyond being marginal, you got to have people who are driven by excellence with a verifiable track record of success to add to the furtherance of the mission— The ideal partnership to meet specific needs.

Let's start right here...the NEED!!

The need? Housing. Dating back to written records in 1909, Public housing was such a critical need that captured the attention of 40 plus philanthropic and religious societies in Philadelphia that eventually birthed the first organized Housing Commission in September 1909.

Some members of the Commission realized there was a direct correlation between bad housing and the contracting, as well as furtherance of the spread of certain communicable diseases such as tuberculosis to highlight one of many. One member was quoted as saying "poor living conditions breed infections and were considered 'evils'". And yes, connected to bad housing....

It was also believed the health ratio would yield more favorable measurements if residents had a proper home environment. What they perhaps considered as proper can most likely be interpreted to include adequate sanitation and ventilation.

Now what is fascinating, not in a superficial way, but in appreciation for those bright minds at the table who knew the value of investing or reinvesting in communities to change the quality of life, understood the possibilities that could be achieved. As well as, living in a healthy environment was linear in determining one's life span. In what most would label as an unsophisticated scientific era, it was widely known that nothing could substitute for quality housing...NOTHING!

George W. Norris, who also became the President of the Philadelphia Housing Commission wrote in his lecture notes from which he talked on March 13, 1913 the following:

"The importance of the subject of housing is such that no apology is needed for the selection of 'The Housing Problem in Philadelphia' as one of the addresses in this course" that was cited in the Catholic Summer School Extension Lectures dated March 3, 1913.

In addition, Norris quoted a substantial finding pertaining to housing by Lawrence Veiller, an American social reformer of the Progressive Era in New York, and a major figure in the Good government and urban planning movements of the early twentieth century.

Veiller fought for and emphasized the urgency of the need to create solutions to eradicate adverse living conditions that impacted children of the poor as well as adults physically, and cited:

"that when the *conditions surrounding* the lives of the poor have been changed, the people have in a large measure changed with them." And Norris continued elaborating in his writings stating:

"Children of the poor are often obliged to live in dilapidated and overcrowded houses in alleys, or 'rears' with inadequate water supply and bad drainage. In order to save these children, their conditions must be changed."

Basically, Veiller was advocating for partnerships. He understood someone, some agency had to take interest and commit financially to alter the trajectory of the poor. To invest in them as valued citizens.

Historically, the planning of the City of Philadelphia by William Penn initially laid out approximately squares of 400 feet long and wide, that included a yard in both the front and rear of the home. The idea was to have suitable housing with provision of some land (grass, perhaps some trees, things that are healthy not exclusively for the environment, but equally to benefit humans) and not have residents boxed in a concrete tomb on top of one another; a model that led to the explosive creation of high rise PROJECTS...

Now, that was a leading concern then, notwithstanding, in our lifetime we know many of the *failed* systems still remain and you have to ask WHY? We know public housing issues are consistently intertwined into the fabric of the national narrative that impacts a plethora of social services, massive funding, lucrative contracts, but sadly, little movement to improve the odds of getting residents out of the PROJECTS. Sure, we have Housing Vouchers and small grants offered to public housing residents, but they are too few considering the case load in government housing.

However, for now, the aim is focused on the GAMBLE that failed in Philadelphia.

Most individuals probably never considered or would have a reason to assess the massive scope of PHA (Philadelphia Housing Authority), nor what it does.

A little background on PHA *(taken from its website)*: PHA is the nation's fourth largest public housing authority, the largest provider of affordable housing in Pennsylvania and an innovator and national leader in real estate development, property management, supportive service, and economic development programming.

PHA has an annual budget in excess of $400 million, assisting more than 30,000 low-income households with approximately 80,000 residents through the Public Housing and Housing Choice Voucher programs. PHA owns, manages, and/or oversees more than 70 multifamily housing developments located throughout the City of Philadelphia including an extensive portfolio of Low-Income Housing Tax Credit properties. As part of its commitment to resident economic empowerment, PHA and its **partners** (***this becomes vital because partnership is paramount***), provide a comprehensive array of services to residents including job readiness, job training and placement, financial literacy counseling, affordable homeownership, and small business development. As one of only a small number of public housing authorities nationwide designated as a ***Moving to Work (MTW) agency,*** PHA is a national leader in the implementation of innovative housing and service programs that respond to the unique needs of the City of Philadelphia and its residents.

So, as you can see Philadelphia Housing Authority (PHA) plays a vital role in supporting, ***purportedly*** improving, and sustaining thousands in its vulnerable population. Well, actually it's a generous gift from hardworking taxpayers, but hey, we are our brother's keeper.

To move the point along, there were countless meetings held amongst the federal government, City Officials, department heads, and community groups screaming for housing solutions in Philadelphia in the 1930s... it is noted; "*those early housing models proved unsustainable as it became increasingly more difficult to provide safe, decent, and sanitary living quarters when the private market failed to produce suitable alternatives*". Of course, most processes were strapped because of the Great Depression and massive evictions and foreclosures that ensued destabilizing the landscape eroded progress for decades. Nevertheless, the people had to live somewhere and we did not have a full safety net in place at the time to prevent total wipe out. Folks found refuge where they could . . . every man for himself.

By the 1950s Philadelphia's African American population soared and was divided into three peripheral neighborhood areas north, west, and south of the urban core. This was during World War II, and two prominent PROJECTS as they were commonly called were built: James Weldon Johnson and Richard Allen Homes (both located in North Philadelphia) specifically for black families.

What is essential to understand is the government got into the public housing business, even reconfiguring shipyards that were once used during the War were funded with federal and state dollars to transform into living quarters for poor whites. Unfortunately, poor blacks were met with the same redlining the private sector imposed upon them ... Whites should stay with whites and blacks ought to stay bunched together with their own kind. Yes, even in the ghetto poor whites were treated a little more humanely than blacks, and other brown people.

Without question there was a lack of private homes to purchase and Public housing in Philadelphia was a significant portion of the overall housing stock...Government ran, government controlled, taxpayer funded. For many, largely blacks who made up approximately 69% of the public housing market, while Hispanics numbered about 26% and 5% White or other there was a conundrum no one seemed to know how to solve or wanted to be solved. At the end of the day public housing needed so many professional services to function as an agency; I mean skilled labor so it would be the perfect match to have unions *married* into the equation.

This brings up the thought as to why a large City like Philadelphia would settle on a model that would call to question the validity of the "Partners" that PHA would later take on to fulfill its core mission to the citizens of the City of Brotherly Love in accord CFR 24.

What would convince Federal, State, and Local Officials to initiate contracts with organizations and private business owners to participate in servicing the most vulnerable in need of a critical social service like housing, without a track record? Oh well, open for business must really mean literally open to do business, and not necessarily with those who should be at the table according to the 24 CFR (Code of Federal Regulations)... Will expound more a little further into the layout of the story.

Nonetheless, the government had a problem, and the folks in charge, the White folks, needed a different approach to handle, manage, oversee, whatever you call it, the poor black people. The dynamics of dealing with people who were culturally different and from an array of educational levels and lack thereof, with little or no money within itself was more than enough to tackle. And having White people do business with blacks in a setting so unfamiliar was akin to oil and water... you were bound to have a lot of movement but nothing would ever coagulate whereby foundational stability could be achieved for extended periods.

So, with hundreds of millions available to allocate to contractors and other professional services how did one of the Philly's native sons become the CHOSEN one to play in this game, when his expertise was writing music? And that successful run dried up in the early 80s.

Many times, taxpayers would take the time to write letters, make phone calls to local, state, and federal officials about public funding allocations and I say to that, it's commendable that someone knows how to make inquiries to demand transparency and accountability. Because ideally, in the private sector if we need a specialist, that's where we go. We don't go to a dentist for a foot problem, we seek out a pediatrist. So, it doesn't make good sense to have a music mogul in charge of managing millions for housing development projects paid for by taxpayers. Nor, placing a convicted felon, Abdur Rahim Islam whose real name is Julius Jenkins on the payroll and served as the chief financial officer whom the FBI eventually indicted for bribery.

Of course, the water is murky already and probably will turn charcoal black by the conclusion of this unbelievable fallacy of a concerned devoted religious figure head who perpetuated nothing less than abuse and fraud.

However, we still have to ask how did Mr. Gamble get here? Where did the opportunity derive from and who protected the UNIVERSAL endgame?

There is no doubt that the money faucet flowed smoothly for them but how? And WHY? Were there kickbacks to officials, union members, gangs? WHAT? Inquiring minds really want to know... There's a well-documented paper trail and ironically as it is public knowledge most of the executives surrounding Kenny Gamble have been indicted by the FBI and awaiting trial, but seemingly his response is he had NO knowledge of any wrong doings. In other words, he is shocked by the recent findings of his long-serving executives who did absolutely nothing without the boss's approval. He ran a tight ship.

According to an article published by the Philadelphia Inquirer a 43-page indictment was handed down charging Islam, (CEO), and Dawan (CFO) with racketeering conspiracy, wire fraud, and tax evasion stemming from more than $500,000 they allegedly embezzled from Universal over a two-year period.

Unequivocally, we cannot sidestep the other obvious fact: Universal Companies was a newly formed entity. How did it qualify to participate in management contracts worth millions of dollars – who opened the door?

0In all fairness it is not usual for government agencies to take on private partners, but usually those partners have experience in the field... So, we will use our imagination at the moment and surmise that there were conversations floating about who could become the ideal partner to deal with the  blacks in the housing projects. Seriously.

It was known that a principal from the nonprofit group The Universal Companies that was formally created in 5/9/2002 according to Commonwealth of Pennsylvania records was vying for a seat at the table as a shareholder, or lead voice to handle the housing crisis in poor black communities, in particular Southwest Philly, his old stomping ground.

Ironically though, in an internal memo dated May 11, 2001, titled Management Planning Meeting with 7 individuals present, there was no mentioning in specifics about existing housing projects under its management. Though the memo frequently alluded to questions or unspecified statements about how to implement the

"Management Plan". Along, with small talk about job descriptions, Community outreach and financial updates.

So, I was asked to described the uniqueness of the partnership model with Universal; what makes it different? Why are they at the table? Here goes:

It is unique because, the white politicians were under the assumption that Universal Companies ("Universal") and Kenny Gamble, and Rahim Islam, and Shahid Duawan being an African-American company would understand, help and support low income Black people because this was the population that bought his soul music and repopulated while listening to his platinum hits.

Universal sold to white funding sources that they could service low and very low-income communities better than any white non-relatable out of touch white person, group, or organization. What makes this unique is that they scared white people into staying out of the desolate, overrun with drugs, high prostituting communities, as if they could change the course of these communities.

In addition, Universal found out after taking the money that just being black was not enough, they called the white cops on the community, they set and made deals with the white Developers, and did not train nor retrain any of the black men and women to participate in the revitalization of the new communities. Get this, the very construct for which they were given a seat at the table, these fine folks systemically blocked, overlooked, fired, and cheated the same class of struggling black people it vowed to help.

.

It all seemed good... Now, what could possibly go wrong? Just hold on, your head will turn.

Let's go back and visit the backdrop in Philadelphia, many Urban areas were desperately in need of more housing; adequate housing to be exact for its low-income residents. During this time there was a surge to create better living models for families residing in public housing, and to get rid of the poorly managed and dilapidated buildings that were not fit for human occupancy. So, as one can imagine the government was open for business and needed to do something different because the aged buildings were becoming more of a death trap and detrimental to the physical health of the residents (these were concrete jungles).

To individuals not familiar with the intricacies in providing access to public housing and managing not only the brick and mortar but the people, and all that comes with them; the psychological and emotional fallout can often register off the Richter scale.

I don't think anyone would argue something nice, not a palace, but suitable housing should be made available to everyone. With that said, we had a number of entities, personalities, clergy, brokering conversations about the need to have housing for Philadelphia's poor. There was a real concerted effort to find solutions.

Just take a glance at how many public housing facilities exists, and some now demolished in Philadelphia and intelligently explain how a music mogul with no housing experience obtained several lucrative contracts. And we'll get to them in the next chapter.

- Passyunk Homes South Philadelphia (demolished)
- Tasker Homes South Philadelphia, in the Grays Ferry neighborhood (demolished, replaced by Greater Grays Ferry Estates)
- Richard Allen Homes North Philadelphia (demolished)
- Blumberg Homes North Philadelphia (demolished)
- James W. Johnson Homes North Philadelphia, in the Strawberry Mansion neighborhood
- Riverview Courts South Philadelphia
- Bartram Village Homes Southwest Philadelphia
- Norris Homes North Philadelphia (apartment tower demolished)
- Martin Luther King Homes South Philadelphia (demolished)
- Hill Creek Apartments located in Northeast Philadelphia
- 8 Diamonds (AME) North Philadelphia

- Morton Homes Germantown, Philadelphia
- Abbottsford Homes North Philadelphia
- Cambridge Homes North Philadelphia (demolished)
- Richard Allen II North Philadelphia
- Cecil B. Moore Homes North Philadelphia
- Champlost Homes Germantown
- Haverford Homes West Philadelphia
- Lucien E. Blackwell Homes West Philadelphia
- Oxford Village Homes Northeast Philadelphia
- Sen. Herbert Arlene Homes North Philadelphia
- Spring Garden Homes North Philadelphia
- Westpark Homes West Philadelphia
- Harrison Homes North Philadelphia
- Fairhill Homes North Philadelphia
- Arch Homes West Philadelphia
- Queen Lane Apartments Germantown (demolished)
- Raymond Rosen Homes North Philadelphia (demolished)
- Mantua Hall Homes West Philadelphia (demolished)
- Haddington Homes West Philadelphia
- Mill Creek Plaza West Philadelphia (demolished)
- Falls Ridge Homes East Falls

- Wilson Park Homes South Philadelphia
- Paschall Homes Southwest Philadelphia (demolished)
- Liddonfield Homes Northeast Philadelphia (fully demolished)
- Carl Mackley Houses, Juniata (now privately owned apartments)
- White Hall Commons (Red Brick) Northeast Philadelphia (Frankford)

Somebody please help me see the connection. As I mentioned, I'll delve into more of the shenanigans in the next chapter.

3

IS THIS SHIT REAL?

With so many multimillion-dollar contractual opportunities on the table the allure to pros and cons was irresistible. I mean, those who understood the contracts and how to service them with timely deliverables hey, fine; you're in business to get more contracts. Now you should know the good book says, "When I would do good, *evil* is always present". And this was not an exception to that... you had those with some experience, not much, but some in housing at the table. Then you had folks clearly from left field trying to hit a home run when they weren't even in the same ballpark of intellect, expertise, and sadly, with operational integrity. You just can't make this up. Though the grave mistake the powers-that-be made was leaning on ASSUMPTION. Some were given a pass and extended invitations to private settings where their façade was still intact, and government and union officials presumed the best was at the table.

I, as a former resident of public housing, strove to leave all negative, negating factors of my childhood behind and successfully rose to the top and acquired access to my PH.D program, and the journey was interlaced with so many dark pitfalls that could have changed the narrative on any given day. But GOD. And for those who don't understand, those two words, ONLY God could make my success possible.

Therefore, being fortunate enough to rise to meaningful levels of operation where I economically impact the lives of others, which is a tremendous blessing, cannot gloss over the infraction committed in front of me as no big deal. It was a colossal error to allow participation of wolves to openly shear away the hopes and dreams of poor black people and be rewarded financially for doing so. I blame every white person who intentionally looked the other way while poor people were continuously being pillaged by the favorite negro, and are we to believe that nobody knew? Really? Am I to believe there was never any checks and balances in housing, or fiscal responsibility, governance? None of that? Did these processes magically dissolve when

Mr. Gamble was awarded? Somebody help me understand this.

Understandably, the allure of lucrative contracts was the sweet carrot for everyone... even those factions that normally would function in their individual silos except for one as previously mentioned, the unions. Anything of considerable dollar value that requires skilled labor, the union is at the table. So, aside from the obvious, some of the characters really did not and don't belong in prominent seats in procurement. As aforementioned, the unions are the exception to the rule because of the various disciplines, yet the entire process is sustained by a commodity, though no one really classifies it as such but it is and the product is POVERTY.

I can hear you. WHAT! Yes, who knew selling POVERTY wrapped up neatly and topped with a bright shiny bow called HOUSING, would be the commodity by which thousands would get rich.

Right here is the perfect opportunity to illustrate what the tangibles are to paint a brighter picture and help you understand why the SELLING of social services on behalf of the poor is BIG business, so this is just a little diversion folks.

If one were to ask one of the bigtime union executives how do you feel about poor people paying your salary; sending your kids to school, footing the bill for that luxury vacation, the expensive jewelry you bought your wife and or girlfriend or both, and let's not forget the other more pertinent needs and wants: poor people put food on your table and gas in the car you drive as well as cover the insurance. That's a lot isn't it? Who knew POVERTY would ever be a life changing commodity, though it is relative which side of the pendulum is in your Favor? However, no one can every honestly say that POVERTY isn't a lucrative line item.

So, what else is in operation? Great question. The players often roll the dice and bet against all odds, cut corners, rob payrolls, shift money and panders political influence but somehow nobody seems to see this... somebody please tell me who's in charge?

As I sat in meeting after meeting and listened to the directives conveyed by the prince himself and previewed numerous schemas of existing projects and future ones, I was so damn stunned witnessing the arrogance of ignorant folk touting themselves as the IT FACTOR. They had all the right moves, knew all the right players, was making significant scores and yet came up morally bankrupt when it came to just taking care of the little people.

The least of them that Jesus Christ was so passionate about and warned the world about: "whatever you do to one of the least of these, you are doing it unto me". And with that said, it's safe to put this in context: Gamble, was abusing Jesus, cheating Jesus, overlooking Jesus, bullying Jesus, and thought it was cool to do so. I'm just putting things in context... His shady deals that hurt the least, the poor downtrodden was the same as stepping on Christ, and there is hell to pay.

When he could have used his vast empire to truly expand the masses because Kenny may be a lot of things, have done a lot things, but being lazy and unmotivated doesn't fit into his world. He had tools, he was a hitmaker, and knows how to influence thought so we have to question why did shit begin to fall apart? And why most did not take the time to count the cost to be in the game is causing the stench to rise and nerves to be on edge.

We all know that shit happens, but can someone please tell me are these black men really that lucky to become a part of mainstream government business worth half a billion dollars without any prior track record? Can somebody please splash cold water on my face I must be hallucinating. Shit happens, and it's getting funkier sooner than later.... By now we know there's a fly in the ointment.

You Mean to tell me….

Will the notable good deeds Gamble has done over his 76 years of life, actually come down to his story, excuse me, legacy being a blip or full-page story "indicted?" Or will some mystical force from the dark underworld arise to save the day?

Several people criticized the writing of this book as being malicious and taking down or smearing another great black man, like the system did to Seth Williams and Chaka Fatah. C'mon man, is there another narrative that's actually relevant to the situation? Like, let's take a wild guess: Whistleblower, you know, something notable? But just in book form.

We're talking about a man who many trusted to oversee millions of dollars though he was not qualified having no experience in the field. I know some would suggest 'well, he knows how to manage money, he was already wealthy'. True, he had money, but what he did not have was the capacity and ethics to be in charge of the People's money.

In addition, no one can convince me that you have a high value target like Kenny Gamble with most of his closest associates indicted by the FBI, and his hands are immaculate ... Nobody, and I mean no one on this planet can persuade any other thoughts I have about that; it is virtually impossible.

Though, Mr. Gamble is renowned for his hard work in the entertainment business as well as his strong arming of artists, writers, producers and even cheating many out of royalties that were signed under his Philly International Label back in the day... Trust me, that person, that business thug did not crawl under a rock, but has blatantly decided to bask in the sun with somebody else's money. Yours.

Let's examine a short list of some of the Real Estate Development projects that Universal is involved with that are all government related (Housing Projects) and CONVINCE me why?

Martin Luther King Plaza Revitalization -65 million – 4-year project to develop 450 units of housing, community center, and community park.

16TH & Federal –$ 13 million – 2-year project to develop 110 units of housing

Point Breeze Performing Arts Training Center - $7 Million - 2-year project to develop a stat of the art 45,000 square foot performing arts training center.

Schuylkill Falls Revitalization - $54 million - -3-year project to develop 330 units of housing and 100,000 square feet of commercial space

Universal Commercial Center - $30 million -3-year project to develop a 150,000 square foot commercial center

Universal Entertainment Complex - $300 million - 5-year project, in partnership with Will Smith (Trey ball Real Estate) to develop 1,000,000 square feet of commercial space and 500 units of housing.

I know these are very lofty projects but let's keep the trek going surely there's more to disclose.

Royal Theater and South Street Revitalization – 200 million – 5-year project to develop 300,000 square feet of commercial space and live theater, and 500 units of housing.

Broad and Spruce - **$250 million** - 4-year project to produce 250,000 square feet of commercial and retail space and 300 units of housing.

Universal Retail Companies -$5 million - 2-year project to develop 45,000 square feet of retail facilities.

Tinley Temple Church – Universal in partnership with Tindley Temple Church will develop the Gospel Hall of Fame, which will be part of the Avenue of the Arts Development

Christian Street YMCA - Universal and the Christian Street YMCA have joined efforts to build a **$4 million Family Center**, which will be an extension of their existing recreation facility.

South of South Street Neighborhood Association (SOSNA) - Universal and SOSNA have agreed to combine efforts on a number of real estate developments, including a 53 units housing development and a 125,000 square foot shopping mall and supermarket

Bethesda Projects - Universal and Bethesda Project have agreed to build approximately 30 one-bedroom apartments as part of Bethesda's mission to tackle homelessness over the next five years.

Cross Street - **$1 million – 10-month** project to develop (7) homes for homeownership

Sheila Brown Project - $1 million – 10-month project to develop 12 single room units for domestically abused women and their families

Beth Tabernacle Church - $4 million - 2-year project is a joint-venture between Universal and Beth Tabernacle Church to build a 21-unit

YouthBuild Charter School - Universal and YouthBuild Charter School have been partners since 1995. Together we have produced more than 25 homes for first-time homebuyers. Our partnership will produce another 35 homes over the next five years.

19th Street Manor - $8 million – 2-year project is a joint venture between Universal an 19th Street Citizen to develop an 84-unit elderly housing development; and

South Philadelphia Coalition – Universal and the South Philadelphia Coalition has begun planning for the development of a special needs housing development at 16th & Moore, former home of a school which has been vacant for more than 25 years.

REALLY FOLKS? Many of these never took off... not even from the piece of paper they were written on.

4

Now you see it, Now you Don't!

When the face cards were dealt with Kenny/Rihiem Islam this started the slight of hand (illusions), one could rule those who were most mesmerized by these incantations were enraptured because they refused to believe the truth staring back at them. Which were men with absolutely no experience in Public Housing management is never a good fit on any day. Without question, if we could create a Broadway Playbill it would read "The Greatest Deception of All" starring Rihiem Islam and Kenny Gamble, and produced by The Universal Companies. The roulette wheel begins the spin of deception in concert with a few of their Islamic cohorts including Nicetown CDC; specifically, ex-felons hired below the prevailing wage to work on government contracts to the tune of hundreds of millions of dollars that exposed the biggest fraud of all.

Nevertheless, some of the high-ranking officials, union bosses, and poor residents in communities drastically experiencing housing insecurities had misplaced expectations for Kenny Gamble and Rihiem Islam's group to solve decades old problems that they were unlearned, unprepared and unfamiliar with.. Unfortunately, the officials/politicians were relying on them to be the fixer, but they would eventually prove to be the grim reaper of hopes and dreams as they stole opportunities and wasted taxpayers money to benefit their LEGACY, and the United Islamic Movement.

Here you have these persons who presented themselves as being the go-to-people a solutionist, or social engineer of sorts who could lead the charge to eradicate the plight but unfortunately poor African Americans in many cities suffer from this sleight of hand by gamblers particularly in Philadelphia.

What made Kenny different in the eyes of many was his success at leading Philly International Records for decades as a hitmaker; he was charismatic and driven. And it was that persona he used to parlay to get a stake in the *public* housing business.

Some of the biggest mistakes could have been corrected only if there was somebody who actually cared… For instance, the lack of understanding of the 24 CFR (Code of Federal Regulations) was a huge demerit. Universal had no knowledge of the 24 CFR, 990, 963, 964, 135.5, and 84.5, so they did not come into the game knowing that the Policies and the Procedures.

They were to include residents to the greatest extent feasible, and participation in the HOPE VI Grant, based upon the charrette/meeting and the Philadelphia Housing Authority were supposed to hold Universal accountable to make sure they fulfilled the obligations of the self-sufficiency of residents with the Section 3 job placement, job training, entrepreneurial development, GED and Workforce prep, credit repair, first time home owners program and the relocation back to the new development.

There should have been metrics in place to measure the effectiveness of Kenny Gamble and Universal's management of the self-sufficiency allocation and HOPE VI Tax Credits.

So many officials bought into the con, however, without a doubt only a few were actually blindsided by what is eventually coming to light in the federal indictments against some of Universal's former personnel and demonstrates gross negligence and misappropriation of federal and state dollars.

The handwriting was on the wall incredibly early; even former Mayor Ed Rendell mentioned to me he realized it was a mistake letting Kenny have participation. Neither was this sentiment a secret to Michael Nutter, another former Philly Mayor.

As noted in a memo from the Schuylkill Falls Tenant Council president dated October 24, 2002 addressed to then Mayor Nutter, it highlights numerous violations of the Universal Companies… rather than rewriting, we decided to just include an actual copy of the MEMO.

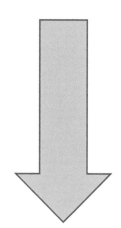

Melvin Prince Johnakin

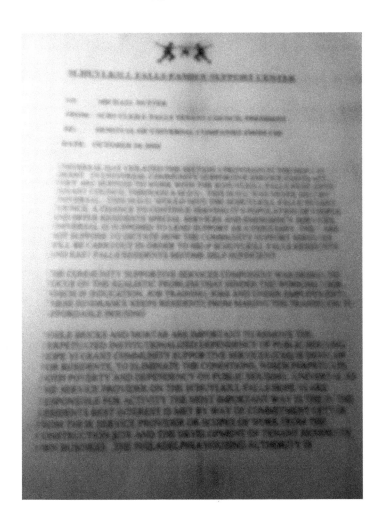

Schuylkill Falls Tenant Council

October 24, 2002

This is a letter to inform the following of the laws that have been violated by Universal Companies. Universal Companies has failed to performed to a signed contract to help assist the Title VIII, Title VI Community Social Service for the Schuylkill Falls residents.

1) Universal Companies has failed to further develop program goals, objectives, or implementation plans for Schuylkill Falls Residents.

2) Universal Companies has failed to provide program oversight and resistance to resident linkage for Schuylkill Falls Residents.

3) Universal Companies has failed to identify and secure commitments of additional resources for the Schuylkill Falls Residents.

4) Universal Companies has failed to provide resources for child care services for Schuylkill Falls Residents.

5) Universal Companies has failed to provide resources for construction related training and credited loan for Schuylkill Falls Residents.

6) Universal Companies has failed to identify what budget is being used to service the Schuylkill Falls Residents.

7) Universal Companies has failed to further resident employment opportunities at the Schuylkill Falls site.

8) Universal Companies has failed in fostering the tenant and residents owned, assist the tenant and residents to become self-sufficient.

9) Universal Companies enable the residents to participate materially in the of modernization per suited to section 3.

Copy to:

Kenny Gamble, Chairman of Universal Companies
Abdur-Rahim Islam, Universal Companies
Carl Greene, Philadelphia Housing Authority
Yaranda Crawford, Philadelphia Housing Authority
Ed Rendell, Former Mayor of Philadelphia
Rick Santorium, Senator
Michael Nutter, City Councilman
Arlen Specter, Senator
Chaka Fattah, U.S. Congressman

My disdain for some of the operational procedures was never a secret, I questioned many who fought to block any significant progress taking place at the grassroot levels where poor people could have been transitioned out of the **Public Housing,** but it was the **elephant in the room** no one wanted to sacrifice. Having single mothers trapped with their children was the credit card with no limits... it paid for a lot of luxury.

Sadly, too many personalities intentionally disrupted real progress from taking place and to this day, mothers and their children are still living in **different locations of the poorest, unsafe, and unclean Public Housing** as a result. When funded **line items were exhausted by Universal Companies management, by hiring Universal employees who worked on other Universal projects and lack of fiscal responsibility,** so went the jobs that were supposed to be created as a part of the Family Self- Sufficiency (FSS) Program.

This **FSS** is a voluntary program intended to help families in **tax credit Public Housing developments get work, keep work and increase their** savings. Any housing authority can participate.

As with **many Public Housing programs** there are pros and cons:

1 It can help families get access to job training, jobs, and job-related needs such as childcare and transportation.

2 As people's income increases, it allows them to put some of their rent money into a savings account, which they get when they complete the program or which they may be able to use for first time home ownership.

The biggest con is that, under some housing authorities' FSS policies, Section 8 residents who fail to follow the program might lose their Section 8 assistance. Under the law, this cannot happen in public housing.

Now, let me take the guesswork out of your pondering how do I know this; I was a professional service contractor and held many longtime relationships with numerous entities connected to PHA, and the HOPE VI Grant Program. And for those who are not familiar with HOPE VI Grant Program, it was developed as result of recommendations by the National Commission on Severely Distressed Public Housing, which was charged with proposing a National Action Plan to eradicate severely distressed public housing.

The Commission was created to service a multifaceted management model; it had concentration and recommendation of revitalization in three general areas: physical improvements, management improvements, and social and community services to address resident needs.

My professional contract put me in the room with the gamechangers; former Mayor and Governor Ed Rendell, Republican Senator Arlen Specter, former Chief of Staff for Governor Rendell, John Estey and CEO of Pennsylvania Housing Finance Association Brian Hudson . . . these personalities initially had faith in having a person of Gamble's stature participating in helping poor African American people struggling with housing insecurities could possibly be a win/win paradigm.

We have to be realistic about the difficulties in managing not only public properties but also dealing with various other negative social elements, domestic violence, drug use, and drug selling, and robbery in economically devasting communities. It was purported that Kenny Gamble and Rahiem Islam were notorious for calling the police on Public Housing residents — I guess one could say was they trying to clean up or root out the bad seeds. Really?

Kenny Gamble/Rihiem Islam were seen as a trustworthy stewards, Chairmen to some, just an all-around great statesmen for the little people; after all that's part of the mantra that got him in the High Stakes door with some government and union officials in the first place.

Let us take a look into another angle up the chain of command in HUD; Alfonso Jackson former Secretary of HUD is now in the mix with the Universal Companies. Well, that's not small potatoes because Jackson is a kind of straight forward guy; a leader with a moral compass and definitely compassionate no matter what media blunders have occurred having an audience with Romney is noteworthy. Alfonso, after meeting with Kenny Gamble was fired from his position at HUD. We cannot guess in the dark, the exchange with Gamble and the Universal Companies had to be egregious for the then Secretary to lose his job over a meeting. Or was it more than a meeting?

With that said, Gamble, for all it is worth made a tremendous name for keep with Philly brand in music and is a charismatic guy. But folks we still need to understand why was this magnet such a force in Public Housing and getting government contracts to provide social services especially in association with the HOPE VI Grant Program.

He was not a builder. Okay, maybe he was qualified as a consultant for the HOPE VI Grant Program under HUD? . . . NOPE! Nothing to see there either folks. As a matter of fact, the Relevant

Experience needed according to Position Objective in order to provide business support for the execution of business services on projects while meeting organizational, business, management and performance objectives required . . . well, I rather you see it yourself:

Do you see 3 to 5 years related commercial or government consulting experience. Though, I think we should start with the 1st line: Bachelor's degree in Real Estate Development/Planning Public Administration

Relevant Experience
♣ Bachelor's degree in Real Estate Development/Planning/Public Administr
Development/Business Management or equivalent in related work experienc
♣ 3 to 5 years related commercial or government consulting experience
♣ Experience leading a small team (2-4 people) to successfully produce qua
♣ Community Development experience preferred/desired
♣ Experience in the following HUD Program offices:
 o Office of Public and Indian Housing (PIH)
 o Office of Community Planning & Development (CPD)

These are some of the requirements to participate so how did Gamble get in? It is just a question folks. The above list is just a fraction of what the HOPE VI Team was supposed to bring to the Roulette table, and clearly none of the above are in Kenny or Rihiem Islam's resumes.

In an article published in The Public Record dated June 10, 2010 the headline reads: 400 Minority Businesses Attend PAPSA Jobs Expo. We are talking about entrepreneurs – women and men of all ages and ethnic backgrounds to learn how to apply for contracts with state-related agencies at a Small Business Expo sponsored by The Pennsylvania Association of Public Service Agencies (PAPSA).

Ameenah Young, the CEO/President of the Pennsylvania Convention Center was overheard telling some that most did not know how to do business with them; "It has been a mystery on how to do business with us. We're here to eliminate that mystery." And since the Public Housing Agency was also present during this Expo, it would not be hard to imagine newcomers at the table trying to learn the nuances of getting in the game.

The article points out the then PHA Executive Director, Carl Greene, brought an initiative together ….

Brought together through the initiative of Carl R. Greene, Philadelphia Housing Authority Executive Director, the group's mission is to actively recruiting other state-related agencies who share their mutual interests.

Carl R. Greene, who is also PAPSA president explained "Bidding for contracts at public agencies is different than contracting in the private market. We wanted to help these contractors learn the ropes so they can get more contracts, and so that we can have a bigger pool of high quality contractors to work with."

Although it is commendable the Housing Authority took an invested interest in helping minorities have a seat at the table, we welcome openness. But what is in question, the same nonperforming organization, not only had a seat at the table, Universal was the table.

5

Some Gambles were Duds

The Universal Companies (UC) by this time had developed a lucrative portfolio of various projects and definitely had the attention of Officials who were very comfortable continuing steering projects their way or accepting proposals for services. Any way you cut it UC consistently secured MILLIONS in contracts with the City of Philadelphia for a plethora of projects.

Over time, deterioration began to manifest on colossal levels as greed and the inexperience of some executives, managers, and consultants became more obvious that adversely affected the financial wellness of its employees, contractors, and a few others.

It is believed that the existing structure whereby Universal Companies operated sent morale plummeting and disrupted the creation of hundreds of jobs. Not just with the housing project contracts, but also with its Charter schools and a few other entities that had received local government contracts. There is no dodging the elephant in the room, the subculture created by the top brass fostered corruption from within, which eventually came to light by the Fed's investigation and subsequent indictments. One can only surmise the operation was protected by external kickbacks and hush money for it to go undetected for so long. There is no question the group had some measurements; some objectives were met and perhaps this is why or how so many of the other objectionable things were kept quiet. Some officials really did choose to believe their lying eyes as to why procedural checks and balances went out the window.

Oddly, in 2012, one would have to wonder who brought content to the attention of Philly's news outlet CBS regarding questionable fiscal dealings – there was money in the bank so what was causing the disruption?

Back in 2012, CBS Philly broke the story with the heading: **RENT-FREE ride ending for Kenny Gamble's Charter School Company**. What!! Now, what could this possibly be about... what rent-free ride? For a Charter

School? Everyone should know operational costs is part of the funding allocation to pay fixed costs like, RENT!

CBS Philly reported the School District of Philadelphia was ending is rent free space to Gamble's Charter School after it had not paid anything for over 1 year. Then-Superintendent Arlene Ackerman had an oral agreement with Gamble and perhaps presumed the native son would honor it. During this time, many had high hopes for the partnership, but as it turned out Gamble's group had to be pressured repeatedly to give up the money for operational cost going forward for the next year for two locations: Audenried High School and Vare Middle School.

In addition, a newspaper article stated, "The company, founded by music mogul Kenny Gamble, has paid zero this year, though reportedly under an oral agreement with the Ackerman administration" but this is not what Ackerman thought she signed up for in the partnership.

At this time, the School Reform Commission was put in a tough spot to now function as a collection agency to get

Gamble's group to pay its debt to the already cash strapped education system of Philadelphia. It was reported that then District Deputy Chief for Strategic Programs, Thomas Darden, had talks with Gamble's group about the money and conveyed to the district it would be issuing a check very soon. Well, it was to the tune of $500,000 for a one-year license agreement according the article.

For starters, what is seriously a sign of gross negligence is money was already given to Universal Companies for its Charter School, so who would authorize occupancy without rent? I am certain you and I know of no one who can stay anywhere or let alone operate a business and collect checks to do so, and not pay rent. Even though someone quoted it was not unusual for the District of Philadelphia to subsidize a charter school's operating costs, it was however, unusual for a charter to pay NOTHING!

One of the advertising slogans for Universal Vare STEM and ARTS Academy is "to foster transferable skills through STEM and Arts programming that will prepare scholars for academic success now and in the future".

Pretty impressive, huh?

Every sensible thinking person knows something is seriously wrong with all of this; the roses aren't that red, and the water isn't that clean, something is really FUNKY and we know it.

Let's go back to March 2011 when the Philadelphia Inquirer released the story: "**Philadelphia teachers union files suit to block firing of outspoken Audenried teacher**". To help you keep the dots connected Audenried School (a very troubled, academic low-performing school) was eventually assigned under management to Kenny Gamble's Universal School Group. The union was protecting the job of one very outspoken teacher, Ms. Hope Moffett, who at the time was 25 years old, and a third-year English teacher.

What is so significant about this article is in the federal law suit it outlined a subculture of intimidation, and corruption, and yes, I am sure you guessed it, people without the proper qualification to take over the school in the first place. Hint, hint anyone? I'll quickly move this segment along but just to give context, at the time Audenried School was in serious financial trouble and had substandard academic performance ratings; definitely not a school you would select as your first choice to send your child.

Anyway, Hope Moffet, being white and well educated, broke her silence about the black and brown underserved children in the school. And as one of her punishments she was relegated to what was described in the lawsuit as a storage area where she was forced to be alone and isolated.

The reassignment of Moffet was called a rubber room – it was considered "unprecedented" by the union for the district's swift removal of Hope Moffet and her colleague from their original classrooms. But it must be accentuated, the teacher, Ms. Moffet never received a negative evaluation prior to her speaking out against Universal

Companies taking over the school. The lawsuit also cited a subculture that ripples throughout other ventures associated to Universal Companies S.O.P. (Standing Operational Procedures); its culture...

Folks, we need to also incorporate into the story that Gamble's group was awarded the school management contract for both Vare and Audenried, and its new $60 million building... In the Philadelphia Inquirer's article, it listed that the Department of Education had already awarded a $500,000 planning grant and thought by selecting Universal Companies, "saw it as an opportunity to leverage those dollars from the federal government". In other words, it would be a sure BET!

However, as time passed, there were other gambles that did not add up for Universal Companies not only in Philadelphia, but also in Milwaukee Public Schools. Who knew the music industry could leverage these types of connections in academia, especially for a man who never secured his own formal education? Gamble, as earlier mentioned was a school dropout.

Since 1993, Gamble, along with Islam both who are founding members of the nonprofit based in Philadelphia initially purported its focus on charter-school operations and developing affordable housing in Philadelphia. This is according to the Philadelphia Inquirer's story. However, with regard to nonprofit status or even being a registered entity in the Commonwealth of Pennsylvania according to state records, the entity filed Universal Companies in 2003, there is a 9-year gap in the math.

This chart was included in an early chapter as well.

I don't want to confuse the issue with fancy language so I'll ask in a simple question. If the organization is purporting to have been established in 1993, why does the state corporate filing list a creation date of 5/9/2003?

I know there are some great mathematicians out there so, somebody please help us do the math to understand the legal standing of Universal Companies to be in a position to participate in managing nonprofit projects prior to its official filing date in the Commonwealth of PA in 2003? Though it purports on its website its nonprofit was founded in 1993. Huh?

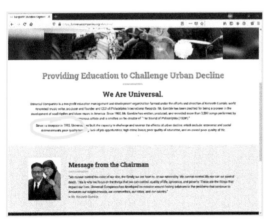

Universal Companies operates seven charter schools in the city: Universal Institute, a traditional charter school in Southwest Center City, and six former low-performing school District schools that the district turned over to

Universal to manage. Okay. Here is the inquiry; WHY?

Again, according to the reported story, the company's financial health was under serious scrutiny after it laid off school staff, and office workers before the end of the 2015-16 school year, which prompted then-City Controller Alan Butkovitz to raise questions and concerns about the nonprofit's management and payments made to related companies, but the company failed to pay its personnel.

Also, two months before the end of the school year Universal laid off school staff and central office workers. As well as sent a memo to employees saying that it needed to "alter" remaining employees pay schedule, to be paid at a later time for a week or so with a promise to repay it before the end of the summer. This was back in early 2017.

As one could imagine this was met with great hostility and pushback that the memo was rescinded and it was noted Devon Allen, a spokesperson for Universal, said the "memo was an accident issued in error".

Nevertheless, the layoffs were confirmed but not the number of employees released, and neither was it ever disclosed how employees' paychecks would be amended.

It is imperative to provide as much concrete information as possible that demonstrates gross negligence time and time again, though with different entities but they all have the exact leadership at the helm, Mr. Kenneth Gamble. Even back in 2016 Universal almost lost the contract with the City for Audenried for failure to meet academic and financial standards. So, I hope to God I can finish this book without losing my mind because there most pertinent question on the table still needs an answer; how in the hell did this person continue to get management contracts?

Now, let's visit the Milwaukee school situation for a moment. Gamble, Universal, and the now indicted and yes,

I forgot to mention convicted felon whose real name is Julius and not Islam aggressively maneuvered to expand Universal's interest in Wisconsin and began bribing Michael Bonds, former board present of Milwaukee Public Schools to secure a lease renegotiation for one campus that would allow the nonprofit to defer $1 million in payments it owed the district. In the federal papers it was disclosed, routine kickbacks were paid to secure benefits for their charter school operations in Milwaukee.

What is known about the setup is according to federal records Islam and Dawan allegedly paid Bonds $6,000 for approximately two years (from 2014-2016) in checks disguised as payments for textbooks from African American Books & Gifts, a company the Milwaukee school board president created. I guess there's nothing to see here folks. However, in federal court in Philadelphia Michael Bonds was charged with *conspiracy and violations of the U.S. Travel Act* through what is known as a criminal information, a charging document employed when a defendant has agreed to plead guilty before a grand jury indicts him... according to contributing staff writer Maddie Hanna.

The feds raided offices of the CEO of Universal Companies in November 2017 and though Gamble has not been mentioned in any indictment as of yet, one still has to look at the cesspool of corruption surrounding so many folks associated with Universal and he claims not to know anything.

How are the taxpayers to feel at ease with this firm securing the people's money when you have executives purportedly without knowledge of fiscal activity? And this leads to my next question; can somebody please tell us Philadelphians who in City government gave Universal Community Homes all these contracts... Keep in my mind, Kenneth Gamble is at the helm so in essence the contracts were given to him, but why?

Well, I wish this was the absolute conclusion but their's to the GAMBLE... in the next chapter it will deal with two distinct problematic contracts:

Martin Luther King Revitalization 65 million 4-year service contract and the Schuylkill Falls Revitalization 54 million 3-years.

6

.The Perfect Dichotomy

The trail of deception with The Universal Companies reads like an episode from the former ABC drama "How to Get Away With Murder", and for those who know the truth and have remained silent it is the deadliest weapon of mass destruction deployed to extinguish hope.

We should not discount that injustice is always perpetrated by complicit minds when you do nothing, or say nothing, because inequality will persistently dominate and rule displaced people without means. In addition, for persons already feeling marginalized, the theft by deception increases oppression and gives an insatiable level of control to those in charge. It is like weaponizing a beast, and the biggest weapon in the hands of the oppressors is the minds of the oppressed.

Specifically, in this case, those most affected by the tyrannical rule were the little people; at least 135 of the residents in some of the public housing system, and few teachers at the Charter Schools were the victims who suffered at the hand of the oppressive, deceitful culture at The Universal Companies. If someone spoke up, they were fired, or if they were fortunate enough to remain employed the environment was so tainted by suspicion and mistrust that it canceled out any opportunities to effectively implement a positive work environment.

Emphatically there were so many missteps and bad policy decisions made earlier enough to put a pause to some of the practices if Kenny Gamble wanted to. He knew everything because that was the nature of the environment, but sadly, many of the recommendations and warnings were ignored.

I can speak professionally to this because my contract was terminated after sounding the alarm to high-ranking officials about the gross negligence, and noncompliance of Kenny Gamble and The Universal Companies. It was so easy to just do the right thing. They had huge budgets so hiring a proficient team was not an issue, but the top brass intentionally cut corners to pocket money for other external and non-related ventures for which the grants/contracts were awarded.

Without question the federal indictments highlight operational and material weaknesses (*breakdowns that happen when there is lack of proficient oversight*). And within The Universal Companies the Feds Rico charges against Islam and Dawan (see the indictment) – you have to question how is it possible Kenny Gamble had no, here this clearly, NO clue this was happening. It is ludicrous.

Here is a snippet from the IRS's Charges:

"IRS-Criminal Investigation is proud to have provided its financial expertise in this investigation," said IRS Criminal Investigation Special Agent in Charge Guy Ficco. "We, along with our law enforcement partners and the Department of Justice, are committed to aggressively investigating individuals who engage in corruption, tax fraud, or other types of white-collar crimes."

"What we have here is four people pretending their motives were purely civic-minded, when, in fact, they were unlawfully conspiring to enrich themselves," said Christian D. Zajac, Assistant Special Agent in Charge of the FBI's Philadelphia Division. "As alleged in the indictment, Abdur Rahim Islam and Shahied Dawan stole nearly half a million dollars from Universal — money for themselves, and to use as bribes to further their financial pursuits. Councilman Kenyatta Johnson accepted their payoffs and based his official actions on those bribes, with Dawn Chavous providing him cover. The FBI is committed to fighting public corruption at every level, and we would ask anyone with knowledge of wrongdoing by public officials to call the FBI or share the information online at tips.fbi.gov."

"As alleged in the Indictment, Universal Companies, including its real estate and education arms, constituted a RICO enterprise, hijacked by the defendants Islam and Dawan to engage in a pattern of criminal activity that spanned two states and several years. In pursuing their criminal objectives, Islam and Dawan bribed public officials, including Johnson, with Universal's funds, and hid those bribes as consulting fees paid through Chavous' consulting firm," said First Assistant U.S. Attorney Williams. "These charges are based on a pattern of activity which violates multiple federal and state laws including mail fraud, honest services mail fraud, honest services wire fraud, wire fraud, obstruction of justice, bribery, and use of an interstate facility in aid of racketeering."

SPECIFICS:

Bribery and Honest Services Fraud in Philadelphia

Islam and Dawan are charged with engaging in a corrupt scheme in which Philadelphia City Councilman Kenyatta Johnson and his spouse, Dawn Chavous, received payments in excess of $66,000 in exchange for Johnson using his public office to take official actions to benefit Islam, Dawan, and Universal, including but not limited to: introducing and voting upon spot zoning legislation related to the Royal Theater, a property formerly held by Universal, and blocking reversion to the City of Philadelphia of another property held by Universal after it failed to develop the property pursuant to its agreement with the City of Philadelphia;

Bribery and Honest Services Fraud in Milwaukee

Islam and Dawan are also charged with engaging in a corrupt scheme in which Michael Bonds, the former president of the Milwaukee Public Schools (MPS) Board of Directors, received approximately $18,000 in exchange for Bonds using his official position to take a series of official actions advantageous to Islam, Dawan, and Universal, including but not limited to: advocating for and voting in favor of Universal's expansion of charter school operations in Milwaukee, motioning the MPS Board to lease MPS property to Islam, Dawan, and Universal, motioning the MPS Board to approve more favorable lease terms to the benefit of Islam, Dawan, and

Universal, and voting in favor of the more favorable lease terms;

Theft and Embezzlement at Universal

Also, according to the Indictment, between 2010 and 2016, Islam drew significant sums of money from Universal in the form of bonuses and travel or expense reimbursements, in addition to his annual salary. Although Universal's Board of Directors was charged with reviewing and approving Universal's financials and major initiatives on a quarterly or annual basis, defendants Islam and Dawan used their positions as CEO and CFO, respectively, to pay themselves bonuses without the approval or knowledge of the Board. Islam and Dawan paid themselves annual five-figure bonuses even while Universal was hemorrhaging money due to the failed charter school expansion in Milwaukee.

The Indictment also alleges that Islam and Dawan used Universal's funds to pay Islam excessive, inflated, or outright fraudulent reimbursements for "travel" or other purported "business expenses." Islam would pad his "expenses" related to the operation of Universal, including its charter schools, with a variety of personal expenses that should not have been reimbursed. For example, Islam submitted his personal car insurance, political contributions, personal vacations, and gym memberships as "business expenses," which were reimbursed by Universal and also not included as income on his IRS Forms 1040. Islam's "reimbursements" were reviewed and approved by Dawan outside the standard procedures for Universal and without proper and detailed supporting documentation. Islam and Dawan also authorized Islam to receive large sums of "pocket money" or per diem from Universal. In total, Islam and Dawan stole approximately $463,000.

If convicted as charged, the defendant faces the following statutory maximum sentences:

Islam: 303 years' imprisonment; 3 years supervised release, a $4,350,000 fine, and a $2,100 special assessment;

Dawan: 285 years' imprisonment; 3 years supervised release, a $3,750,000 fine, and a $1,500 special assessment;

Johnson: 40 years' imprisonment; 3 years supervised release, a $500,000 fine, and a $200 special assessment;

Chavous: 40 years' imprisonment; 3 years supervised release, a $500,000 fine, and a $200 special assessment.

The Internal Revenue Service Criminal Investigations Division and Federal Bureau of Investigation conducted this investigation. The IRS and FBI received assistance from the Department of Education Office of Inspector General. Assistant United States Attorneys Eric L. Gibson and Mark B. Dubnoff are prosecuting the case. Trial Attorney Ivana Nizich of the Criminal Division's Organized Crime and Gang Section in the Department of Justice provided assistance.

This is a twenty-two-count indictment that includes a wide-range of racketeering conspiracy and related crimes: bribery, honest services fraud, multiple counts of wire fraud, and tax offenses according to the IRS Criminal Investigation.

If disclosure of the aforementioned were/are emphatically denied by Kenny Gamble, the CEO/Founder of The Universal Companies, and if found to be true, the lack of awareness points to gross negligence in his leadership. He is the **BRAND**, the *face*, and the golden one that politicians felt comfortable transacting business with for government contracts. And let us put this in context in terms of how many people are at the top; the company's top executives and management team does not consist of hundreds, but a few hand-selected individuals, his fellow Muslims, at the helm of the ship. Okay, no harm, no foul. But no one can convince me that a progressive leader in charge of half-a-billion in contracts does not KNOW what is going on; not on any day of the week can you actually make me believe this. C'mon man.

The inner dealings of housing, school contracts, and purported Workforce Development (the latter being totally obliterated) never fully producing what it was originally designed to do should not be taken lightly. I said it before, and it will be a consistent related theme "Taxpayers paid for this".

We should not overlook the goodwill invested by officials, private partners, and the community who really needed a working model to help assist the most vulnerable get a second chance in life, and to get out of crime-ridden projects, and concrete jungles that are as toxic to one's soul as drinking acid. There are so many psychological demerits to allowing people to live in the Projects; crime is often under reported, domestic violence is also a prominent issue, and petty theft, and not to mention selling of narcotics that lends to a waste pool of unhealthy living environment. And with that said, we have to continue to peel back the layers as to why the oversight in housing projects throughout the United States often come under investigation. As well as Charter Schools. This is a *universal* problem!

Folks we cannot afford to allow fraud and thievery committed by companies and/or their representatives to not face justice. We have a disastrous system in place and people locked into it and pawned at the expense of keeping an operation financially solvent that should have closed. The ratio of millions of dollars allocated for projects that turned out to be bogus is a *tapestry of evil*. Too few were helped though the money was given.

We cannot have a system that consistently spend and spend without accountability or exit ramp to move recipients from *total* dependency to a plan of self-sufficiency. Just so that you are aware, the latter is a model component of PHA that was setup to provide this type of opportunity, but few were successful in navigating because those in charge did not do their JOB!

I can hear some say, yeah, it is hard to help some people, and if you did not have projects or other public housing where would the poor live?

Great question. And I am saying considering the billions of dollars invested and yet spent into public housing programs it is critical for the government to take time to reassess the existing model, again. We cannot continue to shuffle families from one location to another without a bona fide exodus strategy.

Needless to say, when you have individuals who consciously set out to defraud and take from a construct that was created to help the disenfranchise, it leaves a bigger hole and society will continue to spend bad money after bad money.

7
The Culture

Obviously to every person the word Culture, has a different connation, and certainly it is a subconscious directive as to how one should think, behave, and contribute to the world based on its influence, oppression by, or loyalty to the "culture".

Make no mistake in thinking culture is not innate, it is learned. It is fluid, adaptive, and wields a two-edged sword. For some, the culture is a springboard to massive exposure and opportunities to garner wealth, and the flipside, and there is always another side to everything, there is a path strewn with shattered dreams, low self-worth, and hopelessness.

There is a culture in politics, religion, academia, finance, media, and even ethnic culture that influences the behavior of so many whereby they function as a group instead of being governed individually by conscience and conviction. Which is why we occasionally have colossal problems where no one speaks up, stands up, or crosses the line to defend the innocent, weak, poor, and abused. The chum that attracts vultures, sharks, and wild foxes is neatly packaged and wrapped in glitterati; the predators, who lie in wait for an opening to devour, and they do.

What we have here in the Philly Roulette is a high-stake gamble that consistently led back to 1 individual's company whose fraudulent activities uprooted the stems of hope and anticipation for a better future right off the pages of time through theft, and intimidation. It was the gamble that many made, some hit the jackpot, while others were left with broken lives and empty back accounts. And let us not forget who paid for it, taxpayers.

Although, we cannot conclude Gamble did this alone, it would be impossible. The plot was too vast and the machine was well-oiled as to why it almost seemed seamless. There had to be protectors; watchmen on the wall guarding entrances and exists.

As we wrap up I have just a few other notable things to highlight, well, in the form of compounded questions.

How many of you have a private playground where you live paid for with public funding? Or a street that does not allow public parking, but it is a public street? How about a building used for religious indoctrination paid for by taxpayers?

The adage a picture is worth a thousand words still rings true so let's start with a collage and showcase first the beautiful playground taxpayers are generously paying for.

Pretty impressive little piece of real estate; seems safe and well maintained for a public playground, right? Well folks, we really do not need to discuss the rules of this public playground.

No Bare Feet? Hmm. We're just getting warm. Does anybody have a problem with NO chewing gum? Beverages? I can understand **NO** alcohol, but are you telling me you cannot drink water (a beverage) in this playground? Okay, let us define no loitering... well how can one play in a playground if parents and children don't loiter (stroll)?

C'mon folks, these are rules one would post on private property.

A building that was given to the nonprofit became an oasis in which to dwell, along with having a public street cleared with a city ordinance of NO PARKING ON THIS STREET. How is this possible?

Side by side photo

Then former City Council President Anna Verna, gave The Universal Companies this property for $1 that was supposed to be configured for nonprofit activities. Not personal dwelling.

But let's take another look from a different angle....side street view. Look okay, huh? Just another public side street in South Philly.

What? You mean to tell me we get to fund his private, but very public street too? An official City Ordinance sign posted on a public street; why would the City of Philadelphia issue Kenny Gamble an ordinance prohibiting public parking?

Since it is maintained by public dollars, what gives Gamble the right to block traffic to a taxpayer funded street? How much did he pay for this favor? And to whom? The sign didn't just magically appear or post itself.

OTHER TAXPAYER FUNDED GIFTS...

Taxpayers is paying for this building that was originally donated for nonprofit works, not to house a religious faith.

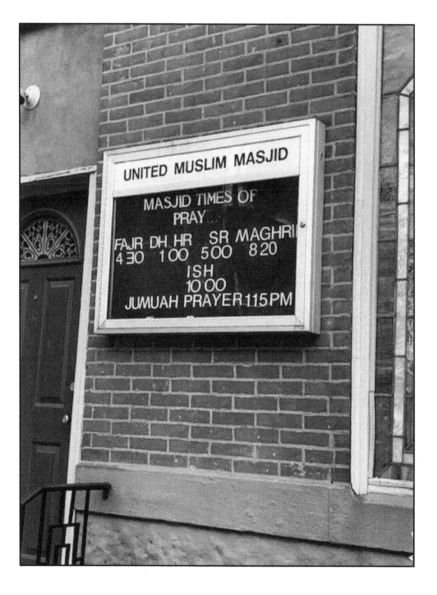

The layout above is heavily surveilled and guarded with limited access... to the far left of this picture is a partial visual of the security guard house adjacent the building. In addition, right next door to the Mosque is where Universal Companies Chief Executive Office and Board President Abdur Rahim Islam resided. The problem with this is the properties were originally supposed to be used for another purpose.

The two locations were definitely repurposed with grants/contract money. We have to do better if poor people are to really get fair and progressive representation to empower them to move from plighted communities where they can have some quality of living.

This book speaks to and uncovers the long-purported lie that black people aren't getting breaks in America; that blacks don't get opportunities to empower their communities and build better models to improve the quality of living. But I guess not when those blacks chosen by white leadership to represent black people are the biggest thieves allowed to blatantly robbed the bank in plain sight.

Just as Justice prevailed in the cases against ENRON, Jeffery Epstein, and Harvey Weinstein, I cannot see the letter of law failing to do the same with Mr. Gamble

Here are the similarities:

- ➤ *Enron – Willfulness to Deceive*

- ➤ *Jeffery Epstein – Charismatic enough to mislead*

- ➤ *Harvey Weinstein – Financially strong enough to be in the game but driven by greed.*

The Universal Companies, led by Kenny Gamble found it easier to do wrong first and play wait and see if they are caught later.

However, I want you to understand I save the best fraud game for last... the endgame in Gamble's mind that he could swindle taxpayers to underwrite and help his future cement his legacy within the Muslim community abroad. It was clever, bold, and extremely ambitious of him to endeavor such an undertaking. Though I would add that folks who helped him along the way, I mean officials, and other private business partners had no idea they were part of an elaborate scheme to rip off the government in the name of religion.

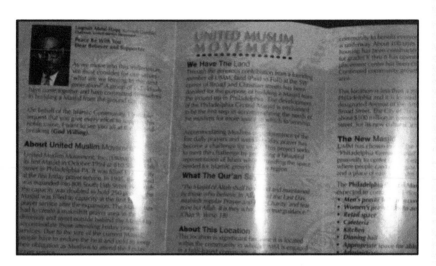

There is one final question and statement; we have all heard of individuals, corporations, and associations fleecing the U.S. government for personal gain, but how many know about a MOVEMENT? When was the last time you read that a religious movement funneled taxpayers' money to further its religious beliefs? Just a question or two...

Is it possible the object of affection and desire was so in your face that everyone looked at it but could not wrap their mind around a religious organization being a hub to defraud the U.S. government? Was this an attempt to take over, push out, or to squash other denominations or was it just GREED, self-entitlement, and possibly a few blacks who felt the White man won't miss a few millions?

These fellas even stooped so low as to use the address where my mother used live in Public Housing as a business address for one of their many entities... As one can imagine I was more than speechless, I am numb.

We must demand accountability... none of the former executives could have single-handedly master minded every aspect of their trail without the top brass knowing about it. We cannot be satisfied until every stone is overturned to investigate The Universal Companies.

Just flawless with one darn lucky gambler at the table who spun the wheel.

The Inquirer 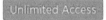 ☰

Execs at Kenny Gamble's charter school operator implicated in federal bribery probe

by Jeremy Roebuck and Mark Fazlollah,
Updated: April 12, 2019

How is it possible for the man entrusted with half a billion dollars not know that the executives he hired were engaged in activities that the Feds deemed suspect?

ABOUT THE AUTHOR

Melvin Prince Johnakin is currently President and CEO of ELT Ventures Inc., a Philadelphia, Pennsylvania economic development and community revitalization corporation with over 25 years of demonstrated success in designing and implementing cutting-edge strategies to provide economic empowerment to America's distressed communities.

Born to a father Longshoreman and a mother of grace, wisdom and courage in a working-class community of inner-city Philadelphia, he saw at an early age what the social ills of America's urban sector would bring in years to come. After losing his father at a young age, his family relocated to Schuylkill Falls, one of Philadelphia's Public Housing developments. He witnessed firsthand urban, social and economic disenfranchisement. Drugs, crime, and poverty were not uncommon elements in his community. Beginning in his teenage years, Mr. Johnakin began to ask, "Why must our community exist under these circumstances? If we are to ever matriculate into a vibrant community of families, then we must own, maintain, and ultimately control the neighborhoods in which we live."

Mr. Johnakin's voyage through the world of entrepreneurship began with the creation of ELT Ventures, a Public Housing resident-owned and controlled holding company that manages various small businesses in Philadelphia, Pennsylvania. Today, ELT Ventures exemplifies the success of cost effectively using U.S. housing program investments and job training to provide financial stability and educational opportunities to distressed communities as a vital part of economic empowerment. The company maintains and manages a sizable portfolio of enterprises providing many services including landscaping, snow removal, general contracting, property management and economic development consulting activities.

He has served as a Project Manager for one of the City of Philadelphia's Public Housing HOPE VI redevelopment projects valued at $52 million. Mr. Johnakin's involvement forced the local Housing Authority, property developers, and general contractors to actively engage in the training and hiring of residents, in accord with Section 3 of the Housing and Urban Development Act of 1968, as amended. He has attracted the ears of those in local government by bringing a source of reason and advocacy to the cause of economic development in distressed communities; this includes testifying before the Philadelphia City Council on multiple occasions. He has served as an economic development consultant for Universal Community Homes, a multi-million-dollar community development enterprise started by world-renowned music composer and legend, Mr. Kenny Gamble.

His professional affiliations include but are not limited to: Omega Psi Phi Fraternity, Inc., Mason Hiram #5 and Shriner Pyramid #1. Additionally, he has been presented with numerous community service awards including the *Men Making a Difference Award*, presented by the former U.S. Representative Chaka Fattah (D-PA).

Mr. Johnakin received a Bachelor of Science in Recreation Leisure Management (Magna Cum Laude) – minor in Sociology from Cheyney University, Cheyney, PA; a Master's Degree Business Systems (MBS) - Concentration Human Resources & Entrepreneurship, from Lincoln University, Coatesville, PA; and is a Doctoral Candidate in Business - Concentration Urban Planning, from Walden University, Baltimore, MD

Melvin Prince Johnakin

Special THANKS to:

Michael Leonardo Graddick, my cousin. He has always
made time to listen and that is all a man could ask from a
great person.

For interviews, lectures or comments contact

ELT Ventures

215 849-2195

CPSIA information can be obtained
at www.ICGtesting.com
Printed in the USA
LVHW070803031120
670441LV00021B/617